Launcelot Andrewes

Masters of Prayer

With foreword and notes by Brother Kenneth, C.G.A.

Designed by Bill Bruce

ISBN 0 7151 0417 9

Published for the General Synod Board of Education
by CIO Publishing 1984

Masters of Prayer

You probably know that feeling of deep pleasure that comes when you meet a stranger who instantly seems like an old friend – whose words are on your wavelength, whose voice is one that you can warm to with immediate affection and what seems like recognition. The people who wrote the words that we have selected for this series of little books are all people like that: strangers from the past who have become the friends of thousands. Their bodies died many years ago, but they live for ever in their words, not as specimens of 'Eng. Lit.', but as *people*, who lived and thought and loved God and understood the problems and the joys that go with being a Christian.

They are usually difficult to meet because they are hidden in thick books and out-of-date language. In this series we have tried to bring them closer, not by watering down what they said, but by presenting short pieces which have the power to speak to us directly and to help our own personal prayer life. We have included photographs too, in the hope that these will help you to discover that the writer's words are still full of meaning to today's very different world.

Use this book a bit at a time. These are powerful words and images, to be thought over and prayed about. The writers in this series are all masters of language; but that is not why we can still respond to them with recognition, why they speak to us over the centuries. They were also masters of prayer. May they be so now, for you, and always.

Pamela Egan,
Publications Officer, General Synod Board of Education.

Launcelot Andrewes

Earthquakes are very alarming events, especially in areas which are not usually subject to them. To the ancients they were invariably a symbol, an almost living symbol, of the fury of the mysterious elemental spirits who controlled the world. And they were naturally afraid of them. In Christian times we may no longer regard an earthquake as visible evidence of the anger of the gods, but it is still a pretty terrifying parable of the consequences of evil and the wrath of God himself.

It must have been so in 1580 when a young man, fresh from university, came to London for a holiday before he entered on his chosen career as a clergyman. He was Launcelot Andrewes and when he experienced, in London of all places, an earthquake that actually destroyed part of old St Paul's Cathedral, he was scared stiff. And that experience must have been a potent reminder to Andrewes of death and judgement all his life. He was then twenty-five and was to live until 1626, but he never forgot it. Like many of his contemporaries he was intensely conscious of death anyway, and whenever he went on a journey he always took his shroud, packed in his luggage. In those days this was not unusual – John Donne the poet and Dean of St Paul's, who must have often heard Andrewes preach, had a statue of himself wearing his shroud, carved for his cenotaph. You can still see it in the present St Paul's Cathedral for although scorched by the Great Fire, it was not destroyed.

Andrewes was a scholar but he also had a great concern for people and it was not long after the earthquake that he was offered jobs in which his talents could be fully employed. One of them was to be a Canon of St Paul's – and there he revived one of the old customs of the appointment by walking up and down the aisles of the Cathedral at stated times in case anybody wished to come to him for spiritual help of some kind.

In 1586 he was appointed to be the chaplain of the Lord President of the Council of the North, and it was about that time that he began discussions with Roman Catholics about the Christian Faith. Later at the command of King James I he entered the lists of controversy with Cardinal Bellermine and Cardinal Perron. It was then, to quote a recent biography of Andrewes, that he began to define "in a new way, where the Church of England stood both historically and theologically".

In 1601 Launcelot was made the Dean of Westminster and when King James authorised a new translation of the Bible, Andrewes, because of his great learning — at the time of his death he is said to have been able to read twenty-one different languages — was chosen to be one of the translators. He helped with the Old Testament section from Genesis to 1 Chronicles. He was a great favourite of the King and when James I was dying he asked that Andrewes come to be with him, but sadly Launcelot was himself too ill to make the journey.

He was made Bishop of Chichester in 1605, following in holiness the example set by his great predecessor, St Richard. It was said of Andrewes that – as a lecturer or teacher he was to be considered 'Doctor Andrewes'; in the pulpit he was 'Bishop Andrewes' (though nobody today would dare preach his sermons in their entirety for they were very long and involved and full of Latin quotations); but in his own room at private prayer he was 'Saint Andrewes'.

It is recorded that he used to spend about five hours each day at his prayers – less than a quarter of his personal prayer book appears here. The complete book he gave to his friend Archbishop William Laud. He had written it out himself, and the editions which have since been printed are usually taken from this book. Unless you can read Latin, Greek and Hebrew at least, you would find Andrewes' own version of his prayers quite useless, but there have been numerous translations, including one in the last century by Cardinal Newman.

When Andrewes prayed he depended a great deal first and foremost on the Bible and then on ancient Christian and Jewish service books. For him it was impossible to improve on Scripture when it came to prayer time. For instance has anybody put in a better way St Paul's statement about our experience of the power of evil in Romans 7:19-20?

> 'The good that I want to do, I fail to do.
> But what I do is the wrong, which is against my will.'

And if St Paul says it so well would it not be a good idea to take his words and make them our prayers? This is exactly what Andrewes did. In his prayers there is hardly a single book in either the Old or New Testaments or the Apocrypha that has not provided him with at least one line. This is a very old way indeed of using the Bible.

So for example, when saying sorry to God for anything that is on your conscience, you might use the words of the Prodigal Son to his father and, as you say them, you will be reminded of the whole story which is about forgiveness. When there are such tremendous words it seems pointless to hunt around for others with these at hand waiting for us to make them our own. Andrewes did not worry that he wasn't a penitent thief nor yet a prodigal son – he took their words to mean what he wanted.

He did not remain Bishop of Chichester for long. In 1609 he was translated to Ely and nine years later to Winchester. In those days the Diocese of Winchester stretched right up to the Thames which explains why the godly bishop lies buried in Southwark Cathedral.

Lord

You are more glorious than the sun
And yet you come to save us.

Light is yours.
     Visible light from sun or fire.
Light of understanding is yours too.

All that we know about you
Lies plain before our eyes:
     – in your prophets,
     – your poets
     – the stories of your people

A light that never goes out.

Lord

Take the blindfold from my eyes that I may see
the marvels that spring from your law:
Turn my heart to longing, day and night,
for your commands to be obeyed.
Make my step firm according to your promise,
and let no worry have the mastery over me.

May I worship you alone!
May nothing ever take your place;
Let me adore you
in the deepest and truest part of myself.
Let me praise you alone,
    with my body,
    especially my speech,
    worshipping with my fellow Christians.

Help me
    to give honour to those who have authority over me,
    and to care and provide for those who depend on me;
    to conquer evil with good;
    to control my body, keeping it pure and treating it
      with respect.

Help me
    not to live for money but to be content with what
      I have;
    to speak the truth in love;
    not to give way to jealousy,
    nor let passions be my guide.

Blessed are you, Lord,

Creator of heaven and earth,
Adored by all your creation.

Bless the Lord rain and hail,
Bless the Lord storms and wind,
Bless the Lord scorching blast and bitter cold
    Sing his praise and exalt him for ever.

Bless the Lord dews and frost,
Bless the Lord ice and snow,
Bless the Lord lightnings and clouds
    Sing his praise and exalt him for ever.

Bless the Lord Angels and Archangels,
Bless the Lord Cherubim and Seraphim,
Bless the Lord you hosts of heaven
    Sing his praise and exalt him for ever.

Lord, Lover of Life

remember your creation for good,
for we are yours.

Christ died and came to life again
to establish his lordship over dead and living:
Whether therefore we live or die
we belong to you.

Father,
by the raising of your Christ from the dead,
set our feet on the path of new life.
Show us where we have followed the path of death,
and give us every good thing we need
to do your will.
Have mercy on us Lord.
Bless us and watch over us,
Be gracious to us,
Look kindly on us and give us peace.

Lord God,

May I adore you with reverence;
Put nothing or no-one in your place;
Neither misuse your Name,
nor be ashamed to admit my allegiance to you.
Make me kind and affectionate, patient and gentle;
Help me to enjoy my body in purity;
Give me honesty and contentment,
destroying in me all unreal fantasies;
jealous hope and shameful thoughts.

Let me continue your faithful soldier and servant to my
life's end.

You are my God

You to whom oceans belong
Seas and lakes, rivers and fresh springs.

Yours is the land,
Continents and islands, mountains, hills and valleys.

To you belong fields and plants bearing seeds,
Herbs and flowers, for food and pleasure and healing,
Trees bearing fruit,
Vines and olives, spices and wood.

The treasures underground also are yours,
Metals and minerals, coal and oil.

You alone are God and Lord,
Glorious over the whole earth.
All honour and blessing be yours.

God,

Sovereign Lord of all,

you loved the world so much
that you gave your only Son,
born of a woman, born under the law,
to suffer, die and rise again.
so that everyone who has faith in him
through the indwelling of the Holy Spirit
may advance in wisdom and your favour
possessing eternal life.

This is my faith.
Help me where faith falls short.

God

You are the one I am looking for
You are my God.

Yours is the Sun who rules the day,
Yours the Moon and stars who govern the night.

> By them the seasons are controlled;
> Spring, Summer, Autumn and Winter;
> By them time is measured;
> Night and day, weeks, months and years.

How clearly they reveal your glory
How plainly they show what you have done.

It is good to give thanks to You Lord
Your love endures for ever.

God of all tolerance

and patience
in your great and full mercy
you are compassionate.

> You take faults away,
> constantly overlook times of ignorance,
> wait many years when we show no fear of you.
> You do not treat us as our sins deserve
> nor does your wrath last for ever.

God of all goodness and grace
in Christ Jesus our Saviour
your kindness and generosity
dawns in love for all mankind.

I will praise you as long as I live,
I will sing to you my God all my life.
Every day will I thank you,
I will praise you for ever and ever.

You Lord

are our Father
yet in spite of your love I do what is wrong
and my disloyalties are many.
I am sold into slavery with sin as my owner.
I can see little good in me.
What I do is not what I want to do,
but what I detest.
I want to do right, but only wrong is in my reach.
My mind whole-heartedly accepts your commands
but there is something deep within me at war with
      all good.
I am almost a prisoner of evil.

Who is there to rescue me?

Though sin is wide and deep
your grace is wider and deeper.
Your kindness leads me to a change of heart,
      I have had time enough in the past to behave
         indecently,
      giving way to my passions in reckless behaviour.
Jesus, who lived and died without sin,
paid the price for me in his blood;

By that precious blood and his Name,
The only Name by which we can be saved,
have mercy and save me.

Father

Let your love rest on us
As our hope rests in you.

The Lord Jesus promises us peace,
    I pray for our peace and salvation,
    for the peace of the whole world,
    for unity and peace in the Church.
Remember all Christ-loving people,
clergy and Christian leaders,
all who live in this home, this town, this country,
all travellers and prisoners, careworn and sick.

Help Lord,
have mercy and save us.

Rejoicing in the fellowship of all believers
especially Mary, more than blessed
Bearer of God,
I commend myself and all my fellow Christians to him
    who can keep us from falling,
and set us in the presence of his glory,
jubilant and above reproach.

To the only God our Saviour
be glory and majesty
might and authority
before all time, now, and for evermore.

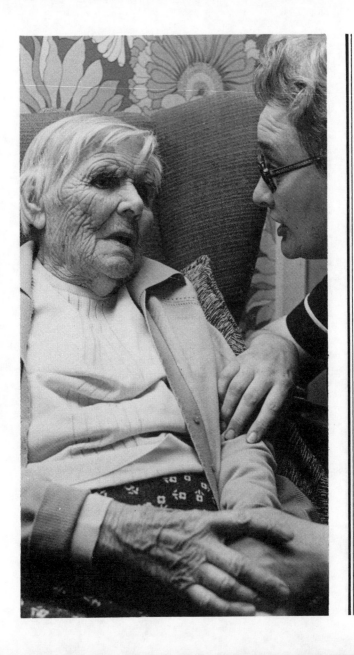

I Exist

I am alive
I have a mind,
    Lord, my Lord, I praise you.

For my upbringing and education,
for my instruction in the Christian Way,
for the qualities and abilities you have given me,
    Lord, my Lord, I praise you.

For the success I have had,
for all the good I have received from others,
for my present situation and future hopes,
    Lord, my Lord, I praise you.

For my parents, teachers, wellwishers and friends,
for those who have helped me by their
    books,
    words,
    prayers,
    example,
    tellings off,
    wrongs,
for the things I remember and the things I have forgotten,
those done because I asked, or without my asking,
    Lord, my Lord, I praise you.

How can I repay you for all your gifts to me?
What thanks can I give
for all your patience and love?

You are worthy Lord
to receive glory and honour and power
for you created all things
and for your pleasure they were created and have
    their being.

Lord God

all glory and all goodness are yours.

> Yours is the earth,
> with every kind of living creature,
> cattle, birds, reptiles and all wild animals,
> waters teeming with life,
> and Man whom you make in your likeness
> to rule over your creation.

Thank you Lord
> for my mind,
> and for those who can see into your mind.

> For my innermost self,
> and my ability to praise you.

> For my freedom,
> and the wisdom of the past which helps me choose
> well.

> For my body, my feelings and my sex,
> and for your laws that teach me control.

Lord Jesus

Fill me with your love.

By the mystery of your Body and Blood
first given to your disciples
on the night before you died;
and through your Ascension into the realm of heaven,
Draw me to yourself.

Jesus

On your cross, and now in my brothers and sisters,
    your sweat like clots of blood,
    your heart ready to break with grief,
    your brows surrounded with a crown of thorns,
    your head beaten about with a stick,
    your eyes filled with tears,
    your ears listening to insults,
    your lips moistened with drugged wine,
    your face befouled with spitting,
    your shoulders bent under the weight of the cross,
    your back, bloody from a savage beating,
    your hands and feet ripped through,
    your voice crying 'My God, My God, why have
        you forsaken me?',
    your heart pierced with a spear,
    your body broken and your blood spilled,
Jesus, remember me when you come as King.

Life of Christ make me holy;

Body of Christ give me strength;
Blood of Christ redeem me;
Water from the side of Christ wash me;
Weals of Christ heal me;
Sweat of Christ refresh me;
Within your wounds, Christ Jesus, hide me,
drawing me to yourself
so that I find in you
    a sure ground for faith,
    a firm support for hope
    and the assurance of sins forgiven.

Lord

By your servant Moses, you led your people to escape
    from Egypt,
So by your servant Jesus you have led us to escape from
    evil:

Your people rested in safety on the other side of the
    Red Sea,
So through the waters of Baptism we your people rest
    from sin:

Your Son Jesus rested in Joseph's garden grave,
So one day I must live beyond death with all who are in
    Christ.

Father

I am your son.
Treat me as tenderly as a father treats his children.

Lord Jesus
you are my Master;
As a slave follows his master's hand
so are my eyes turned to you,
waiting for your kindness.

I believe that if I were neither a son,
nor your servant,
but a beggar,
I might eat the leftovers from your table.

Jesus you are the Lamb of God.
Lamb of God, who takes away the sin of the world,
    take away mine.
You came into the world to save sinners;
    Save me for I am among the worst of them.
You came to save the lost;
    Don't allow to be lost one whom you came to save.

Holy Spirit
you are the Lord and Giver of Life,
    don't let my living be pointless.

You give me life through grace and hope
  and in the sacraments,
   don't let it be wasted.
I believe you come to the aid of our weakness,
pleading for God's own people in God's own way;
Include me in that pleading.

Lord

I know that Christ once raised from the dead
is never to die again.
Let me regard myself as dead to sin,
but alive to you in union with Christ Jesus.

> Add to this my faith, goodness,
> to my goodness, knowledge,
> to my knowledge, self-control,
> to my self-control, endurance,
> to my endurance, holiness,
> to my holiness, brotherly kindness
> to my brotherly kindness, love,

Don't let me forget my past sins have been washed away.
May I exert myself to clinch your choice and calling of me.

How Great and Wonderful
are all your Works

Lord God Almighty,
How right and true are your ways, King of all Nations.
Who will not fear you Lord?
Who will refuse to declare your greatness?
You alone are Holy.
All nations shall come and worship before you,
for your righteous deeds are seen by all.

Praise our God all you his servants,
and all men, both great and small, who fear him.
The Lord our God, Sovereign over all
has entered on his reign:
Exalt and shout for joy and do him homage.

At last God's home is with men.
He will live among them,
and they shall be his people.
He will wipe every tear from their eyes.
There shall be an end to death and mourning, crying
and pain
for the old order has passed away

Lord you are making all things new.
You the Trustworthy and True, the beginning and
the end
the sovereignty of the world has passed to you
and to your Christ
who reigns for ever and ever.

Amen.

Index of first lines

Photographic Acknowledgements

Page 11: *'Snowy Mountain'*, Interfoto
Page 17: *'Mother and Son in Wells Cathedral'*, Reverend Alan Beck
Page 21: *'Old Lady and Friend'*, The Salvation Army
Page 25: *'Two and a Bike'*, Interfoto
Page 31: *'Father and Son'*, Ron Jeffries